ESFJ:

Understand And Break Free From Your Own Limitations

MATTHEW BRIGHTHOUSE

Copyright © 2017

Table of Contents

1
Introduction

The fact that you have picked up this book tells us that you have taken the Myers-Briggs Personality Test, and you have received your result of an ESFJ personality type. If this is the case, you are certainly a popular, caring, and highly social being!

Known as 'The Consul', you are someone who makes up around 12% of the population in your type, and you love to be right there in the heart of any social setting. However, this doesn't make you false, as you are someone who is super-caring, and you only ever want the best for people. You do have a tendency to become hurt quite easily, but overall, you are certainly one of life's good guys. Give yourself a pat on the back!

This book is designed to help you maximize those strengths which are common in your personality type, but also to identify your common weaknesses, and to turn them on their head, changing them into strengths. Every single personality type within the spectrum has its upsides, as well as downsides, and there are some personality types which have more negatives than your type does! The aim of this book, therefore, is to help develop you as a person, helping you to become the best individual you can be, and saving you from situations where you may become hurt more easily than someone else, or from a situation where you may come across wrong to another individual.

Of course, if you have taken the test and you came up with a different personality type, but you also identified quite closely with a lot of the personality traits associated with an ESFJ personality type, it's definitely worthwhile reading this book, as well as the book which is your main personality trait result.

This is because we are all very complex beings, and we never totally fall into one camp completely. You may be a majority ESFJ, but you may share traits with a different type too, and in order to develop yourself completely, to help counteract any negatives and turn them into positives, you should read about both. This will give you the information you need to really deal with any situation that life throws at you, and do it in the most positive way possible.

We should point out that when you read about the weaknesses that are associated with the ESFJ personality type, you should not take anything as a negative criticism – everything contained within this book is designed to help you, to give you everything you need on your self-development journey. There is no part of your personality type is that vindictive, nothing that is particularly nasty, and nothing that is going to make you stand out as a less-than-wonderful person. But, it is important to realize that nobody is perfect too! Weaknesses are part of being human, and if you can realize that you have them, and turn them into positives by developing and understanding them, then you really will break free of any limitations you may be placing upon yourself without even realizing it

After that? The world truly is your oyster!

So, let's stop procrastinating and get onto the good stuff. Prepare to learn all about your caring and social ESFJ personality type.

2
The Fine Line Between Strength And Weakness

So, you have identified that you are a majority ESFJ personality type and that you are The Consul. Every single personality type is made up of common traits, but also of strengths and weaknesses. You will see that every strength could be a weakness if developed too far and that every weakness could be a strength if developed in the right way. This is what makes your self-development journey so interesting and rewarding!

In order to understand your personality type, you need to know what the letters themselves stand for.

E – Extraversion
S – Sensing
F – Feeling
J – Judgement

Let's break that down a little and understand more about each letter and what they stand for.

Extraversion
You are no wallflower socially, you are someone who loves to be right there in the thick of it. You are a fantastic organizer of social events, and you love it when everyone is happy and having a great time at an event or gathering that you organized. You are likely to be a popular person, and you like it that way; ESFJ's are likely to have been the Home Coming

Queen, or the Jock at school, or the head of class etc... Basically, you are someone who likes to be liked, and that can also be your downfall. ESFJ's have a habit of putting too much importance on social standing, and that can lead to hurt feelings on their part if someone doesn't like something they have done or something about them.

We are going to cover this in more detail in a later dedicated chapter, but if you can learn to see past the falseness of social standing and understand that you can't control how someone sees you, that you can only do your best, then you will find that your feelings are hurt much less overall.

On the flipside, however, ESFJ's are fantastic organizers, and if there is an event that needs to be pulled together at the last minute, they are certainly your guy or girl! As an ESFJ, you are not likely to be someone who enjoys last minute plans, you don't do spontaneous; overall, you prefer things to be planned and put together properly.

Sensing

Despite being a very sensitive person, you do not tend to place that much importance on intuition or anything 'otherworldly'. You often find that sensitive personality types are much more based on gut feeling and intuition, but ESFJ's are quite the contradiction. Instead, as an ESFJ, you prefer to stick to traditions, laws, and basically anything which relates to rules and authority. You are not very philosophical in the way you think or make decisions, and instead, you stick to what you believe to be right. As such, you are a very strong believer in 'doing the right thing'.

The problem for an ESFJ is that being inflexible can become an issue. Every single person is different, and that means that we all make our decisions based on how we are brought up, our traditions, our culture, our customs etc. As an ESFJ, you need to try and understand that your right isn't necessarily someone else's right. If you can learn to do this, you will see that your decisions are much more easily received by others and that you will be able to please more people as a result. As an ESFJ, you love to please people, so this will be a great plus point for you too!

Feeling

We have mentioned that ESFJ's have a tendency to be sensitive, and this is certainly the case. You aren't weak by any means, but you do like to be able to put a smile on someone else's face. And that, in turn, makes you feel appreciated. You take criticism very harshly, basically taking it right to the heart, whether it is meant that way or not. In order to be able to be less affected by criticism, and to be able to see it as constructive, rather than always intended to be negative, it's important to be able to identify the positives in it too. This isn't always easy at first, but we are going to dedicate a separate chapter to this important issue in the ESFJ world.

In terms of friendships and relationships, you are certainly someone who is warm and welcoming to anyone in your life, and you love to make sure that everyone around you is doing okay. You could be described as a gossip, but that isn't in a malicious way; for you, as an ESFJ, your interest in the lives of others is more about checking to see that everything is okay and that nothing is wrong, and not meant in a malicious, or nosey way. Obviously, those who don't know you well could take it the wrong way, and this is something to be a little cautious of from time to time.

Judgement

ESFJ's make their decisions based on traditions, laws, and rules; they are not people who think creatively and bend the rules, they are people who are always by the book of morality. You do have a slight tendency to be judgmental towards those who don't think in the same way as you. We mentioned this earlier, but understanding that what is right for you, isn't necessarily what is right for someone else, is vital. Someone else could be making their decision based on their own morality, just as you do, but their right and wrong are slightly altered compared to yours.

Now we know what the ESFJ personality type is grouped together as, at its very core, we need to move on to look at the common strengths and weaknesses in more detail. It's important to realize that not every single person who received an ESFJ result is going to have every single strength listed below, and similarly, not every single ESFJ is going to display all of the weaknesses. Personalities are very complex things, and this means that you need to look at the parts which do adhere to you, and then look even deeper to see if the others are part of your makeup and that perhaps you're just not aware of it.

It's a good idea to have a chat with someone close to you, someone who knows you well and asks their opinion on the strengths and weaknesses associated with the ESFJ personality type, which you're not sure you exhibit or not.

Let's look at strengths first of all.

ESFJ Strengths

Very Practical

You are the ideal person to have around when something requires organizing, and that is why you are often found to be the person organizing events, social gatherings etc… Basically, you're likely to be the ideal person to go to when it comes to putting these types of things together. You do have a slight tendency towards going a little too far sometimes, e.g. you want to please and achieve, so you put a little too much time into the organizing side of events, perhaps to the detriment of yourself sometimes. This is an area to work on, and something to bear in mind if you find that your time is quite limited to spend on yourself, and you're always organizing and arranging things for other people.

A True Team Player

You are someone who works very well with other people, and you love nothing more than achieving something together as a team. You are not someone who is selfish or someone who wants to grab the glory for themselves, and instead, you gain a greater sense of achievement from your team's success. Your team members are also very appreciative of your fantastic organizational and practical skills too.

You Always Do What You Say

You have a sense of duty that is very strong, and that means if you say you're going to do something, you do it. You can basically be relied upon to get the job done, and done well; this is why you are likely to be a very valued member of any team you are working as part of. You are loyal to a fault too, and you are not somebody who will let anyone around them down if they can help it at all.

A Warm and Caring Person

You are very sensitive, both to yourself and to the needs and wants of others. This means that you are caring and warm, and you want other people around you to be comfortable, thriving, and happy. If someone has a problem, you are always a great person to go to, and you will do whatever you can to help that person in need with whatever problem they have.

A Social Butterfly

You do not find it hard to connect, as a very social being. You love being in groups of people, and you thrive when there is a true social setting. You come across to others as a warm person, because that is exactly what you are, so there are never any issues with people thinking you are cold, unfriendly, or otherwise. Again, this means you are ideal as an organizer of social events.

ESFJ Weaknesses

Very Concerned With Social Status

You are not happy if you are not liked or appreciated, and you place a high amount of importance on being high up in social circles. This is not because you are vain or cold in any way, but instead, it is because you thrive on being needed. You want to know what everyone is doing, not because you are being obtrusive or nosey, but because you want to know if everyone is okay, or if you can do anything to help. The problem is, it doesn't always come over to other people as it is intended, so sometimes, ESFJ's need to be careful that they are not seeing as being intruding.

Unable to Cope With Plan Changes

ESFJ's are not known for their flexibility, and they do not like to make plans at the last minute; instead, they like order and in advance plans, which are always stuck to. Whilst this is good in a way because it means that everyone knows what they are doing and when it does suck the joy out of life in other ways because spontaneity can be fun too! If you can learn to let go a little and to be a little more flexible in terms of your planning, you will be a little less uptight and will be able to go with the flow much easier.

Very Keen on Their Comfort Zone

Working hand in hand with the last point, ESFJ's do not like to go out of their little comfort bubble too often. ESFJ's like what they know and change can make them nervous. We are going to talk in more detail later on about this point, because learning to take risks and perhaps edge a little out of your comfort zone one step at a time, can yield some fantastic results, and some great experiences overall.

A Tendency to be Needy

Because ESFJ's want to please people, and because they are so sensitive, this can sometimes come across to others as being too needy. In some cases, this can cause the other person to back away, which has a damaging effect on the feelings of an ESFJ even more. Learning to hold back a little, and not come across to others as needy is something that will really help you to develop yourself as an ESFJ. Your relationships and friendships will thrive as a result.

Put Themselves at The Back of The Queue

ESFJ's are very selfless, to the point where they put themselves last a lot of the time, in order to make someone else happy. Whilst there is nothing bad about wanting someone else to be happy and to see them smiling, it does matter when you are the one suffering. Again, we will talk about this in more detail later on, but learning to put yourself first occasionally, is a must, and it will never be seen as selfish.

As you can see, ESFJ's are very caring and kind people, but that comes at a price – putting yourself last can be damaging. We are going to talk in each chapter about the main points you can work on, in order to develop yourself and make the best of your ESFJ personality type. As you will have seen from this chapter, there is nothing hugely negative in your particular personality makeup; you are someone who is liked by most people you meet, you are sociable, and you are kind. Celebrate those positives and hold them, dear, before working on the negatives, for a truly successful self-development journey.

3
Learn to Realize That We Are All Different

We have mentioned that ESFJ's make their decisions in life based on duty, law, rules, and what they believe to be right. They are strong and upstanding members of the local community. Now, how do you decide what is 'right'?

Every single person has their own set of opinions, and they also have their own idea of what is right and wrong. Whilst most of us agree of the most important things in life, e.g. cheating in a relationship is wrong, hurting someone is wrong, lying is wrong, there are other areas where it all becomes a little more grey. This is where the ESFJ can call into murky waters.

The thing is, when making decisions and forming opinions, it is important to listen to your gut and to understand that your own set of beliefs is important. We have developed our own version of right and wrong from our upbringing, our culture, where we have come from, and our own experiences in life. This is what has shaped us as people. Now, every single person comes from a different place in life, e.g. a different country, a different culture, a different house, a different city, a different upbringing, a different social standing, and that means that we all have a different version of what we believe to be true and right.

ESFJ's are quite inflexible when it comes to plan making, but they are also quite inflexible when it comes to understanding differences too. This doesn't mean that ESFJ's are intolerant, far from it, but sometimes there is a tendency to not understand that their version of right isn't necessarily someone else's.

Of course, we're not talking about the big things in life here, such as whether killing someone is right or not; of course, these things are no-brainers, but we are talking about decisions in life which are based on morality and ethics. An ESFJ isn't judgmental, but when dealing with the belief system of someone who they can't get their head around, they can it all totally confusing.

So, how can you change this and turn it into a positive?

Learning About Our Differences

Basically, as an ESFJ, it's important to realize that we are all different and that this is a wonderful thing! It would be very boring if we were all the same – can you imagine? We all thought the same way, we all believed the same thing, we all wanted the same things; life would be dull, there would be no debate, no fire, no passion, everything would just be flatlining.

If you can understand and embrace the wonder of this, ESFJ, then you will be able to deal with the decisions of other people who don't believe and think the same way as you. Of course, you might still roll your eyes, wrinkle your forehead, and think 'why?', but you will also understand that they have made that decision based on their own beliefs and rules, and not based on some far-fetched idea. Similarly, other people might look upon your decisions and wonder why you have made such a choice, but provided you know in your heart that you made such a decision based on what you believed to be true, and the rules and regulations that you hold dear, then there is no discussion to be had.

Understanding this point is really about a mindset shift in yourself. You are not considering yourself to be better than anyone, and you are not belittling their thoughts or beliefs, it is simply that as an ESFJ, you are so stuck on rules and regulations that your morality doesn't allow you to accept differences easily. You are such a believer in your own set of ideals that understanding someone else's can be hard. The bottom line is that you simply need to accept that everyone thinks in a different way – you don't need to understand it, you simply need to accept it, shrug it off, and continue on your way.

The beauty of life comes from the fact that we are all exotically and wonderfully different from each other, and that brings forward a whole host of possibilities. If you can understand and embrace this, then you will be able to understand other people around you much more easily.

4
Learn to Realize That Criticism Can be Useful

From reading this book so far, and from understanding yourself, you will know that as an ESFJ, you can be quite sensitive. You are sensitive to the way other people feel about you, you are sensitive because your feelings can be hurt easily, and you are sensitive to the feelings of others too. Because of this, you are particularly open to becoming hurt quite easily.

Other personality types, perhaps a harsher type who isn't as emotionally open, will probably hurt you without even realizing. It's important to realize that they probably don't even mean to do this and that they are in fact simply speaking their mind, without meaning to upset you in any way. The problem is, as an ESFJ, you find criticism hurtful because you take it so personally. So, having said that, if you find this book to be hitting any nerves, please know that my intention is only to help increase your awareness so that you can live as your best self. Oftentimes, you are so concerned with how people view you, and what they think, that any slight criticism can be very hurtful to you, and can linger in your mind for a long time afterward.

The problem with that, ESFJ, is that you are concentrating on a negative that really needn't bother you much, if at all. Not all criticism is intended to sting or hurt, and most criticism can be used as a tool for growth.

For instance, if someone says to you that they enjoyed the event you organized, but they didn't really enjoy the food, is this a direct reflection on you as a person? Of course not. You probably didn't even cook the food. You arranged a wonderful event, which the person even said they enjoyed, but instead of focusing on the compliment they gave you, instead you focus on the criticism.

Another potential example here is a relationship. If you are in a romantic relationship with someone who isn't as sensitive as you, there can be a battleground of hurt somewhere in the middle. You are hurt quite easily, but the other person doesn't realize this. A comment about your outfit has the power to ruin your evening, but the other person probably never even intended it that way, or even thought much about it.

How to Deal With Criticism

The problem here is that you should never rein in your sensitivity because it is part of who you are; it is what allows you to sense when someone else has a problem that they aren't telling you about, and that is what allows you to help other people as much as you do. What you can learn to do, however, is learn to take criticism in the way it is usually intended – constructively.

Ask yourself whether the person is really being mean or negative, or whether they are simply voicing their opinion, which they are entitled to do, and whether there is a hidden compliment in that perceived criticism. If you look hard enough, you will usually find one somewhere.

The next time someone gives you some kind of criticism, whether it is intended to be criticism or not, instead of thinking about the negative and becoming upset about the words, flip it around and ask if you can use it as a springboard for growth or improvement. For instance, the comment about the event that was great, but the food wasn't wonderful – simply don't use that catering company again! As for the outfit comment, was it really meant to hurt you, or was it just meant that they preferred another outfit on you because that other outfit really showcases a part of your body that they like? Don't see the negative all the time, try and see the positive. In addition, as we mentioned previously, most criticism has an underhanded compliment in there somewhere, you just need to dig it out and find it!

Of course, there are some people out there who will hand out criticism simply for the hell of it, and it is intended to wound and hurt. These people have the issue here, not you. It's really about confidence, and if you believe in yourself, if you love who you are, and you know that you are doing your best, that's really all you can do. As we become a little older, this does become easier, but for some people, confidence is always a slight issue. You can learn to conquer this by building yourself up and not listening to those who try to knock you down.

As long as you do your best in life, what else can you do?

5

Learn to Step out of Your Comfort Zone, And Embrace Spontaneity

How do you feel about being spontaneous? As an ESFJ, it's not likely to be something you practice very often, and when you are forced to engage in being spontaneous, you are likely to find the whole experience quite uncomfortable and distressing, until you settle down and realize that it wasn't all that bad in the end!

As an ESFJ, you have fantastic practical and organizational skills, and when you are arranging and organizing something, you like it to run like clockwork. This is because you place so much importance on social status and standing, and you don't like anything to upset your plans. If something causes a problem with your event or plan, you worry that people are going to think badly of you, but that's not the case!

Embracing spontaneity is something that as an ESFJ, you can really work on. You will find that as you allow yourself to go with the flow a little more, a whole world of opportunities begins to open up, and you will feel much more relaxed as a result. We know that you are not someone who finds it hard to socialize, so allowing yourself to see where the flow takes you is never going to put you in an awkward or difficult situation socially.

Your Very Cozy Comfort Zone

A comfort zone is called that because it is literally very comfortable. We find relaxation and ease of comfort, and it can become very addictive. The problem is, comfort zones ca be quite damaging in many ways. If you don't venture out of your zone on occasion, you could be missing a whole host of opportunities. Not everything in life has to be planned out. Nature teaches us a very important lesson about life – nothing ever stays the same. See change and breaking out of your comfort zone as an exciting opportunity for growth.

Have you ever heard the old adage that the unplanned nights out are often the best? This is because you don't have expectations, and you don't have time to build it up in your head to be something amazing, only to find that it wasn't really all that amazing in the end. Expectations are the root of disappointment, and when you are spontaneous, you don't allow that disappointment any time to creep in.

The fact that ESFJ's are so concerned with what others think is usually the reason that spontaneity is not often embraced. This is why plans are stuck to, because plans are comfortable and easy, and with plans, we know that everything is going to work out as it should do. The thing is, problems do happen, and instead of becoming upset about it, taking it all so personally, it's important to just roll with it, allow life to occur as it wants to, and just adapt as you roll. Nobody is going to think any less of you because you didn't plan everything out from time to time!

Of course, you can't be spontaneous every single moment of your life, and there are times when plans need to be made, but the main area of development for an ESFJ is to allow life to occur occasionally, and not to be upset when you are forced to be flexible and change course. People will judge you no matter what you do in life, whether good or bad, and really all that matters is that you are pleasing yourself, those you love and care about, and that you are doing the right thing. As an ESFJ, it's very unlikely that you are going to go around breaking laws or rules, so you know you're on course in terms of doing the right thing!

In terms of your social arrangements, those events that you are so good at pulling together, you have a tendency to become very frustrated, or even angry, when something doesn't go according to plan. This is where you need to develop a sense of humor and laugh at life! Have faith that it will all work out in the end, as it is supposed to do, and that you cannot control the things in life that are thrown at you seemingly randomly. Think of yourself as a problem solver, thinking on your feet and rolling with the punches. If you can find excitement in that, if you can find a real thrill from doing so, then you will be able to accept that random things happen on occasion much easier, and it won't ruin your day to the extent that perhaps it does at the moment.

In terms of giving this spontaneous thing a go, just try it once, just once. You'll see that being spontaneous can be fun, and whilst you might not want to embrace it every single second of your life, you won't become worried or upset in the future when you are forced to go with the flow again.

6
Learn to Put Yourself First Occasionally

You might be wondering why it is a weakness to put others first, to be selfless and to cater to the needs of others. If you are thinking that way, you are displaying your true ESFJ nature!

Whilst there are no major downsides in caring about others and wanting other people to be happy, it is a big downside when it comes at the expense of your own happiness. From time to time, you need to learn to put yourself first and not to feel guilty about it. Is this something that is going to come easily to you? Probably not, but owe it to yourself and your own inner peace to try it occasionally. It's all about balance, you see. Life has to be about pleasing everyone else and pleasing yourself at the same time, although you should certainly only ever try to please the people that are important to you.

As an ESFJ, you are always on the lookout for your friends and family, and you are often trying to find out what is going on their lives. This is not out of being nosey, although some people can occasionally see it that way, instead, it is about wanting to know that they are okay, that everything is going well, and that they are happy. When they are happy, you're happy.

Some would describe you as a gossip, but it is never meant with malice. You are a gossip in a good way, a person who spreads good and joy. If you can learn that you need to give yourself time, as well as giving it to everyone else, then you will be able to find a true balance in your life.

When your life is out of balance, nothing really feels right; you might try and fill that by focusing on other people, but you are actually doing yourself more harm than good. Other people want you to be happy, just as much as you want them to be happy too. As an ESFJ, it is important to think about yourself as much as others.

The Art of Saying 'No'

Have you ever been asked to do something, which you really didn't want to do? We're not talking about something you had no choice in, e.g. a work task, but instead, we're talking about a friend asking you to do something and you didn't want to. For instance, maybe you were so tired from a very busy week at work, but your friend asked you to babysit so she could go out for dinner with her husband. You didn't want to do it, in fact, you had a million other things to do at home, and you were feeling exhausted. Did you do it? You probably did, because as an ESFJ, you would have been more concerned with making your friend happy, and you wanted her to think well of you too.

Now, the correct answer to that situation really should have been that you gently and politely said no, but that you would babysit for her in a day or two. You should put yourself first in these situations from time to time, especially when you are feeling wiped out and tired. Self-care is vital!

It's important to find a middle ground here because you don't want to be going around saying no to everything!

As an ESFJ however, this is unlikely to ever become the case. You want to be like, as we have said time and time again, but if you are not feeling great about yourself, how can you be expected to help anyone else?

Try it once, and don't give in when you start to feel guilty about it! The first time, this is bound to happen, but embracing the fact that you need to show yourself some love is vital. Saying 'no' occasionally is not about being obtrusive or difficult, it is about assessing the situation and coming up with the best solution for all involved; occasionally that best solution is about you, and not about anyone else.

7
Learn to Hold Back a Little

We have mentioned at length that one of your key strengths as an ESFJ is the fact that you are very warm and loyal, you are someone who is super-sensitive, and although this can be both a blessing and a curse, you are certainly not going to let anyone down easily. This is one of your major strengths and it is something you should certainly hold dear.

The downside, however, as we know there is always a downside in life, is that this sensitivity and eagerness to be liked and to help can occasionally come across as needy to other people.

This isn't all people, and it is most likely to only be an issue around personality types who are a little less emotionally charged than you. For instance, if you are in a relationship with someone who is much less focused on their feelings, and more focused on logic, you may find that you are hurt quite easily. We talked about this in our constructive criticism chapter, but it is a definite truth for your personality type. That person doesn't mean to hurt you, they don't even know they're doing it, but their harsh words can be interpreted as hurtful to you.

Now, as an add-on to that little issue, the fact that you want to be liked so much, and the fact that you want to help others means that you can go a little too far on occasion. This means you put yourself last, as we discussed in our last chapter, and it can also mean that your actions can be a little suffocating to other people.

The Problem With Neediness

Neediness is never meant in a negative or bad way; someone who comes over to other people as needy is not doing it because they actually feel clingy and desperate, more often it is due to an intense desire to help or make that other person feel wanted. There is never any negative intention, but as an ESFJ, you do need to be aware that occasionally, if you allow your desire to make others happy go a little too far, your overall demeanor can be misinterpreted.

Neediness isn't something that is often seen as a positive trait, so again, you simply need to check how you may be coming over occasionally. You are so sensitive and warm that you tend to give your entire all to another person, and whilst this is certainly not a bad thing, and is actually a wonderfully warm trait, it is something which can be too much for a different kind of person.

So, how can you ensure this doesn't happen?

Learning to Hold Back

Basically, you need to hold yourself back a little. This may be totally alien to you at first, and it will feel very strange, but there is nothing wrong with keeping a little bit of you for yourself only. If you give everything to another person, including your time, then you will probably end up feeling a little exhausted at the end of it too. The other person needs space to breathe, and there is a lot of truth in the thought that if you are not always available, the other person will miss you. This might seem like mind games to you, and something which is a total waste of time, but human beings are complex, and occasionally games do come into play.

Not always being at someone's back and the call will certainly allow them to appreciate what you do for them so much more, and ironically you will feel that appreciation on a greater scale than if you were otherwise just doing everything without much of a 'thank you'. As human beings, we are flawed, and when someone is doing everything for us, we take it for granted; it becomes normal, and we don't see it as something special, or something to be thankful for. If you back off a little, if you allow the other person to really see just what you do, and how you make them feel, you will notice the difference.

Your ESFJ nature will certainly enjoy this extra attention and appreciation because at your very core you want to be appreciated by everyone around you. Only by learning to back off just a little, allowing others the time to really see what you do, can you feel this appreciation in the greatest way possible?

Try these little tricks:

- Don't text back straight away, wait for a little before you reply
- Be a little unavailable, e.g. don't jump and say 'yes' to that invitation straightaway
- Say 'no' just once, e.g. when they ask you to do something that you really don't want to do
- Allow yourself a little 'me' time

These hacks are not hard, and they are actually things you should be doing routinely, putting yourself first on occasion, as we talked about in our last chapter. If you try them, you will see that your neediness is much, much less, and as a result, you are mastering that particular weakness that is associated with your personality type.

8

Learn to Place Less Importance on Social Status

Anyone who masters the art of not caring quite so much about what other people think about them will truly be a happier person as a result. This is a truth. Of course, only pleasing yourself and not caring about anyone else isn't what life is about. But, there is a balance to be found; when you find that balance, life becomes easier as a result.

When you are so concerned with the thoughts of others, second-guessing what they think and feel all the time, how can you be comfortable or happy? Always wondering what something else is feeling, or what they think about that thing you did, or that outfit you wore, is basically exhausting and it is very damaging to your self-esteem too.

You cannot please everyone all of the time, this is a truth of life, and once you learn to accept and really believe this fact, you will be much more comfortable in your own skin too. The only person you need to please really is yourself. Everyone else will fall into line when you know you are doing the right thing by you, and as an ESFJ, you are very unlikely to do anything which isn't considered to be in line with your morality or rules.

Attempting to make everyone happy with your choices in life, and your actions will only ever result in failure. This really harps back to our first chapter of 'learn to' chats, when we talked about the fact that everyone is different. This means that we all believe different things to be true, and we all have a different set of ethics and moral markers. This means that you literally cannot have every single person approve of your every action, it is downright impossible and never going to happen. Trying to achieve the impossible will only bring you down.

Does social status really matter all that much anyway?

This is what you need to ask yourself.

As an ESFJ, yes, you care about what other people think about you generally, but you also care about your social standing quite a lot too. This is really about the example we mentioned at the start – an ESFJ is likely to have been a cheerleader or captain of the football team at school, someone who was always considered to be top dog but not in a malicious or vain way, in a high standing way to help others. If you can learn to accept the fact that you don't need to be high up in a social standing to help others, then you will be able to rid yourself of the shackles of caring about what other people think far too much

The Damaging Effects of Caring About The Opinions of Others Too Much

You might think that it is normal to care about what other people think of you, and to a degree, you would be right, but there are many damaging effects that are associated with this too. If you can understand these, you'll be able to get a much firmer grip on what we are talking about here.

- You will second guess every decision you make, and tie yourself up in knots
- You will not be true to yourself and your own wants and desires because you are too busy being true to the cares of other people
- You are likely to miss out on opportunities that you would have loved to pursue because you were too concerned with what other people thought about it
- Caring about the thoughts of other people is a time-consuming thing, and you will probably tire yourself out in the process

Basically, how can you know what someone else really thinks and feels unless they directly tell you? Many people aren't great at opening up, and you might consider them to think a certain way, but deep down they might not really be of that mindset. You can't read minds, and if you try to, you're going to tie yourself up in knots and drive yourself slightly mad.

Hopefully, you can now see how damaging all of this can be. Whilst there is an admirable part of it all in there, e.g. caring what other people think means that you care about them as a whole, it's important to really understand that you will never please everyone. Making it your life's mission to have everyone like you and approve of your every move is not something to dedicate your years on this earth too. Instead, dedicate your time to making yourself happy, and caring about those who are close to you. This is a much more worthwhile way to spend your life.

9
Conclusion

By now, you should have a much wider view of your personality type overall. You are certainly a popular person in many different ways, not only in terms of the prevalence of your personality type but also in your social circle too. This is a great thing because you will be well-liked, which will call out to the need in you.

Throughout this book, we have talked about your strengths and how to maximize them, celebrated them, but we have mostly concentrated on your weaknesses, giving you the information and know how to develop them and minimize the impact they have on your life.

As an ESFJ, you are not someone who has a whole host of negative traits to work on, in fact, you have very little in the way of traditional negative issues. What you do have however is a few traits which can be tweaked to make your life better, and to help you become much more content in your own life. For instance, we talked at length about not caring as much about social standing and the thoughts of other people. This is a mission you need to work on because this will certainly give you a lot more peace of mind overall in your life. This will certainly free you of the limitations that you are unwittingly placing upon yourself, probably without even realizing it.

Your tendency towards coming over to other people as needy is also something you can put some time into developing away from, as this is going to allow you to feel less unsure of yourself from time to time, and again, will free you of the constant worry of whether someone else is happy, what you can do for them, etc... Giving yourself time and a little care will enrich your life and will give you more time and energy overall.

Remember to check out the personality types which surround yours, especially if you find yourself displaying any of the traits regularly. It's a good idea to read about all personality types, because not only is it a very interesting subject, but you will almost certainly find something in every single one of them that you identify in yourself. In addition, you can work on these issues, to minimize any negative impact, and also allow you to break free from any limitations you are placing upon yourself.

The ironic thing is that by doing this, you will also be able to understand other people much more easily too. For instance, if you can identify from being around someone the type of personality they are, you will be able to understand why they act the way they do, why they make the decisions they do. This will mean you can deal with them in a much more positive way, and you can breed stronger relationships overall. Knowing about people is not only interesting, but it is very useful in life too and can help you meet and understand new people much more effectively as a result. If you are in a management role at work, understanding personality types can also be very useful in terms of people management too.

All that is really left now is to wish you luck on your self-development journey. Remember not to take any of our advice personally, and certainly remember that it is not a criticism in a negative way. We are trying to help you become the best version of yourself that you can be, and if you take on board the advice and pointers we give you, you will give yourself a true shot at ridding yourself of the shackles of limitation. The world is your oyster in so many ways, and if you can embrace your caring wonderful ESFJ personality, whilst making a few modifications along the way, you will be able to move mountains.

Thank you for purchasing and reading this book. If you enjoyed it or found it useful then I'd really appreciate it if you would post a short review on Amazon. I do read all the reviews personally so that I can continually write what people are wanting.
If you'd like to leave a review then please visit the link below:

https://www.amazon.com/dp/B078YHPTKZ

Thanks for your support and good luck!

Check Out My Other Books

Below you'll find some of my other books that are popular on Amazon and Kindle as well. Simply search the titles listed below on Amazon. Alternatively, you can visit my author page on Amazon to see other work done by me.

ENFP: Understand and Break Free From Your Own Limitations

INFP: Understand and Break Free From Your Own Limitations

ENFJ: Understand and Break Free From Your Own Limitations

INFJ: Understand and Break Free From Your Own Limitations

ENFP: INFP: ENFJ: INFJ: Understand and Break Free From Your Own Limitations – The Diplomat Bundle Series

INTP: Understand and Break Free From Your Own Limitations

INTJ: Understand and Break Free From Your Own Limitations

ENTP: Understand and Break Free From Your Own Limitations

ENTJ: Understand and Break Free From Your Own Limitations

<u>ESTJ: Understand and Break Free From Your Own Limitations</u>

<u>ISTJ: Understand and Break Free From Your Own Limitations</u>

<u>ISFJ: Understand and Break Free From Your Own Limitations</u>

<u>OPTION B: F**K IT - How to Finally Take Control Of Your Life And Break Free From All Expectations. Live A Limitless, Fearless, Purpose Driven Life With Ultimate Freedom</u>